Scorched Blue

Siena Chitty

BookLeaf Publishing

India | USA | UK

Presentation by *BookLeaf Publishing*

Web: www.bookleafpub.com

E-mail: info@bookleafpub.com

ISBN: 9789358316513

First edition 2023

That is Love

Listen with intention
And without expectation
To that of the sound of leaves
That are gently brushed by the breeze
Or the brisk walk of beings
That dread the days beginning
You might realise how the rest will come
To you quietly
And as silently as a smile
As woeful as a promise
That has been kept, right here for you
Ideas will squawk from birds that fly
Within the walls that cannot, inside your minds
eye
The sentences you have tried, out on tongue
Your whole life has a set, a cast
A stage it is to become
The script will one day reveal itself
Within the package, that is you
To the outside world that always knew
It all has come from you
Like a summer lover, some truths will float by
like the wind that passes your wings as you fly
high

Knowing you were the person inside the cries
that lied
Just know
That there is more, there will always be more
Through currents that soar within seas that roar
louder than ever before
Life is not meant to be easy
While you ride out turbulent tides
Under weeping skies that live in your eyes
Across borders you never dared cross
Until the sun becomes heavy and hot
The liquid light running through your very heart
And catching fire to the things you cannot bear
to part
You will know
The difference between the ache and the relief
The forgiveness of the weak
You will know
The beauty in falling leaves
That brushes the floor because of the breeze
That is love

Forget to be Holy

I try to sleep but my eyes don't seem to fall
away
I'm just sleepwalking in vain, as I weigh up the
pain
Through these mountains of madness and what it
means to be alive
I can't even cry, I've tried a million times
It is a harsh reality we're told
I'm beginning to forgive myself though
Beginning to commit myself to the flow
In the fleeting moment of life, we seem to be
living it
On the way, we can't quite decide and notice
and we seem to slightly die every time
We do realise
That nothing is really real, in this world, and in
this life
I'll try harder, don't worry
Live longer, be holy and forgotten
Would you give me more of what I need
If ever I needed it though
As I commute to work I try not to meet your
gaze
I can feel the coffee within your veins
The way we slightly say our names

A generation always on the move,
for which I can't seem to prove anything to
You're just a sleepwalking zombie,
a tired overwhelmed wannabe,
for which I have applied all of the love that I
carry
Walking the rest of the way to work
trying to forget the things you say, when you're
not alone
When I am not with you
You seem comfortable though
Let me be some part of your awakening
Falling for what was, in the undetermined future
of what will be
I can finally see, why my eyes don't seem to fall
away in sleep
As I continue to forget to be holy,
you give me the hope I've been hoping for
Inside my mind, I try to find the way we fall
within sleep
Forgetting to be holy and we weep as we sweep
our minds clear
Every time we fall asleep.

Moon Made Of Jealousy

It is a particular kind of hell,
to be put on hold,
and then to be told that the descending sun,
is prettier than a silent moon made of jealousy,
hissing in its torment but still shining brightly.

Without any warning, your time will come,
Signals lead to the door of another floor, the one
you didn't mean to enter,
the one you didn't even ask for
Slightly forgetting how to speak
Entering in its peak
I find this life to be evolving but bleak.

And you know, that a jealous moon is much
more dangerous than a setting sun. In the
delights of what is to come, forever done with
the end of the world,
you slowly slide off of it when the day has
finished.

We know the lover's pain when the tables have
turned and the losers have learnt how to play the
game.

The hollow art of the forgotten, the solid
presence of a feeling resembling longing.

There is knowledge that we give, to people we
don't know,
the ones on trains moving freely through time,
grinning softly but still tentative to the grind. For
they are allowing for rain and for trouble to
regain some grip on the love that they hold. With
which only they can hold, the love we are
searching for is travelling north. It has different
plans, the love we are searching for has
abandoned us and all that we find ourselves in,
like a sea of blue, there just for you.

The jealous moon casts its cold hands into the
darkest oblivion, knowing with immediate
loneliness, that the blankness has other ideas,
only taking what it can't touch, in its
imagination, it can trust that the sun will only
move one of two ways, according to the moon, it
always stays, never strays, near enough to keep
its cool, near enough for the moon to look like a
fool but it will never burn the cool wings of the
moon. Only hurt the feelings fluttering within
the circle that yearns, learns its faults can be
fatal.

For we have abandoned ourselves,

More times than we can know,
We have become stranded and the moonlight has
helped us to grow.

But a moon made of jealousy is something else.
The light that shines has been tainted, nearly
silenced is a moon made of jealousy. If I had a
ladder I would climb to your light, ever bright,
dead of night. I would make your feelings valid,
take the smallest bit of madness and replace it
with something other than the jealousy within
your light, for that way, the shine through the
dark is less tragic and more sporadic.

Your madness will replace its sadness.
While we are forever guided by the moonlight.

Building Site

They are building in here, something I cannot
see.
Yet I can feel them building inside of me,
somewhere regardlessly.
Are they building a new heart, something lighter
to love?
Or are they building me a cage to lock away my
emotions or to one day release the dove, that
lives within my veins? Perhaps a staircase to
overcome my fears.

The building is long, hard-earned work. I
wonder if they get paid enough or if the work
will ever be finished.
Sometimes I can hear them, chipping away at
my soul.
Are they looking for something? Will they find
any gold?

On Sundays they pack up and have a rest,
perhaps this is a test. I feel the most lost on
Sundays. Perhaps they long for the sun to shine
down upon their hands, maybe to be free, and
escape my body for good, I really wish that they
could. Perhaps they don't want to do the work.

Maybe it's just a contract, that I did not sign.
Time will tell, between these fine guidelines.

Despite time, I can still sense them during the
week, working hard and endlessly.
Maybe they're not separate from me at all, and I
know them very well, maybe they know me and
everything in all that I have to tell.

In this life I feel better, the work they have done
has made me feel brighter. It's like they lit a
match and my soul caught fire, in all of my
desires I know it's a good thing. For them to be
working and for me to be concerned.

I do worry a lot, for what of I know not.
But these workmen are kind.
They bring lunch and help me survive.

Wounded Moon

The light stares at me blankly.
The night knows nothing of its hold.
The bright light stares down upon my sadness.
The blankness that I have been told, to keep and
one day meet, the darkness inside my soul.
I have been trying to see myself through.
To better find a way to you.
Held by patience.
And lifted by the light.
That shines upon my sadness.
It's in the fragments of delight, touched by my
intentions, and sometimes taken for a fool.
So much deprivation.
Have you made the cut? Because we seem to
think it's in each of us.
The pain that seeps into the deepest parts of my
heart.
The pain gives us tougher lessons.
That we bide our time by.
They declare themselves every second.
And I have known this, from the moment I
stepped into the cool moonlight, from the point
of no return, in its tragically calm presence.
The darkest nights still have the moonlight.
The comfort it gives, in this moment.

For I want to stay living and give these moved
parts of myself, to the light that seems to be
grieving something we do not understand. Not
now, not yet. But at least I can see you out there.
Wounded moon, what can I do?
I think I have fallen for you.
Wounded moon, are you really there, I see all of
your sorrows in the light that lead me home. Say
it's all alright. But I yearn so tragically,
transparently in your translucent haze. Glazed
eyes.
Painful days, devastating losses.
You knew me, and I knew how to be alone in the
light of your heart.
Heavenly thrown from the depths of this.
I left it still and didn't move for a year.
I kept your heart hidden.
Planted a seed, inside my soul.
To one day be the light that you dissolve.
Forever hold, one day we'll evolve.
In the wounded moonlight.
Forever okay, forever alright.
I stare at you blankly, the power behind my eyes,
I can see the emotion as it will kindly arise.
Wounded moon, who are you?
In the noise of the sky, I know this isn't easy for
you.
Hardened by the fire of the sun.

Looking too closely into the collapsing blaze.
Forever holding its gaze.
Wounded moon, this is all for you.
For we do not know of the ultimate tragedy but
of the times that we got over gravity. And for
this brief moment, we float toward another, the
other, forgery in the light of a thousand nights,
that I still claim, to this day. You are the
wounded moon I see at the centre of my dreams.
The core of all my light. You create it, you have
made it. A heavy wound by the wounded moon
who holds on tightly, brightly, you are the moon
I see, shining down upon my sadness.

In The Forest Fires Descent

We stand so silent in the midst of our wrongs,
we fight so firmly against the rhythm of right.
I catch sight of you hot-tempered in the light,
asking if any of this is permitted?
If it is even alright.
For what has been, remains to be seen because
we can't seem to make any sense of it.
Sensible souls riddle through the gaps of
existence, forever distant.
Not home, not even within reach.
We forever seek what we are deserving of,
In due course, we will get what we were
prescribed.
How can we measure it, in times of forest fires?
Through our pose and troubles, our lunacy
subsides.
Too compacted to contemplate, when we give
people a duration, is it really a vacation?
To abandon the ship and desert an open road.
I have been told that solitude in a barren land of
fleeting madness will subdue.
Will it soften the blow, make me feel any less
low?
My heart can't seem to yield it, make me forever
conceal it.

How wrong, how provocative it is to be in this position.
Where the heat reaches higher levels than I can depict.
The cold diminishes as soon as it gets to that degree.
As the stronger currents abide, my time is running dry.
I am hurt, I am light, so ruthless in these destructive tragic ways.
Maybe it was in the sunlight and its gaze.
I have been hurt by exceptional people, who always mean well.
But did me wrong when I was forever distant, in my vacant body.
Placid atmospheric truths, for I have seen more than I can bare.
Under mountains of despair, even in your tears, i am there.
So unloved and told to be love, but I have never been taught how.
How in a world that is encouraging of love can I not?
These fragments have been blessed.
So unaddressed
Excessively fraught
My time here is up
I even watch the dust, as it falls, as it settles.

Counteracting the worst, in the gorse of the
unloved.
Among the mist of our wrongs, we fight so
firmly against the rhythm of right.
And I can hear you asking yourself, is it alright?

When The Day Has Died

I'll think of you
And when the day decides to go
I hope you'll think of me too
For the evening is coarse so unaddressed
distraught
The morning is for grief, so fragile and
indiscreet
Maybe with some unpleasant disbelief
But with everyday that goes by and slowly dies
Comes with it new opportunity to learn and
grow to give and to know
That love did and has existed all around
You being here, love did know which way to go
before the day died
And my tears run dry
There will always be more
Through unopened doors where sunrises seep
through windows onto tired eyes that are
grieving the day
That do realise that there has been and still is
love all around
When the day has died
And the moments in them subside
In this, the rhythm knows which way it's going

Where the heavenly winds are blowing through
you
When the days die there is not much to do
except reflect
On times you may have lived and on times you
may have not yet
We are either in the past or the future but rarely
in the present of the mind
Falling through time
When the sides of the day collapse in and tumble
down onto you
I hope you find the surface
You are somebody's given purpose
To breathe, to see, to love
When the day has died.

Follow Your Light

The road runs deep, within these subtle tides of
rebellion
As the waves move, the sky reinforces its hold
on the world
And we stop to look, at the crooked path, that
takes us there
Your tears stay dry, if only to release there worry
from the sea
And we fall, further than them all, every time we
hear it
Trying to subside the feelings met, the curtain
call
The road runs deeper, as we try to sleep it off
Scars below the stars above
I've tried to become unloved, but the love we
hold
The faces of a starlight that guides you home
The way all you wanted to do was roam and be
loved
We run deeper down the road of the unknown
Lovingly thrown from the heavens, down routes
only gods can see
Do you see? Because the path to a certain
feeling has become unused
We look again, follow your light

You'll be alright, the ways in which we guide
each other there
Releasing stares that echo and bellow beneath
the heat, the raging wings of eagle's soar
I think I've lost you before
Follow your light, it's the only one that'll guide
you forward and back to the great unknown.
Where we fear the very reason, the very season
of self.

To The Mountain

When the mountain that is your life
doesn't fit the mould you are trying to fill

or the concept of what it is you're about
and it doesn't sit right with your beliefs

You will start to wonder how people can trade
mountains.
How do we overcome obstacles that will make
us?
Thinking that maybe your mountain was
destined for another,
this mountain is a lesson and your name is
carved into yours.
Permanent like ink, when the mountain that is
your life

Beckons you to start climbing
like a tide, you keep going against
like a wind blowing at you and right through
your bones
to where you are going
Or think is a better place.

Trust the mountain's pace

and the climb that takes a lifetime
for the view at the end is different for every one
of us
the view lives in your heart, just before you start,
to fall for
your life, and your climb

Your soul is sublime enough to give you time, to
get through
But when the mountain that is your life
Asks you to push on
I hope you listen to it
I hope you know that with
every step further, every monumental moment
that takes you higher,
it is a chance to get closer to a purpose promised

To a life that was granted, before you were born
To the mountain that is yours alone, and will be
there until the very end

You can make peace with something so
tremendously overwhelming,
and look to each step as an achievement,
encourage yourself to keep going
because when the mountain that is your life, is
there beside you
and it supports and guides you

I wish for you to know what it means
and to recognise it is there, living within a
lifetime ahead.
To the mountain that is yours.

The Receipt

A receipt blows in the wind
Outside the supermarket
Of a truth
I will learn today
I see you at the checkout
There is a woman stood beside you
Yet I still pay with a pain in my heart
Seeing you in another life
Should be a gift, but it is a curse
A vacant receipt still blowing in the wind
Outside the supermarket
Where we first met
And I feel hurt replaying and igniting within me
Because I shouldn't be here
Our lives tremble
and they stand as separate entities
Among the pain that is loss
Mourning for your receipt to be mine too
I know now what I've lost
But there is still hope
For my cart to be full
With new ideas and different memories
Yet I seem to be tragically distraught
My heart terribly caught up
On another receipt that blows in the wind

Vacant is my mind
Every time I try to catch it
Not knowing if it is mine
I paid for this life, just as I have done so with
what I bought here today
Knowing you are free from the receipt of me.

Heavy Silent Air

I had never walked so far in my life
With bags that stayed with me
Under eyes that would fail to see
The light in it
That would fade
and bring rhythms that swayed
Beneath what we both called home
In this heavy silent air
That surrounds us
I had never walked so far in my life, ever
Towards somebody who was walking away
I walked further than I had ever
The heavy bags beneath these eyes that failed to
see
The potential in this, the longing in a world fall
of risk
Brisk days, tragically gone
Let's cause a riot, come in and be quiet.
Talking in whispers until we make our
conclusions, is just an illusion, walk out and use
them. Silent heavy air.

The First Cloud

There is a lot riding on something I know
nothing about
On something I'd like to think that I am
prepared for
That when it came I'd know it well
As an old friend, before time was a thing or this
life gave me any degree of love
A lot is riding on a place I have never been
And a feeling, I don't often feel
For when people ask what it is or what I'd like it
to be
Sometimes I don't tell them, I tend to go down
paths they can't easily see,
between lines of trees and places of greed,
touching neither, knowing both.
I sometimes say that the beginning will always
start closest to the ending of something else, that
the two are actually lovers, distantly infatuated
with one another like the sun and the moon,
frightened of the darkness that does exist
between the spaces that hold them together, like
the blue and black of the night. Gentle, ever
close. Always parting ways or saying hello
like they can't differentiate

between entering and leaving, beginning or
ending
like they can't love like usual lovers
Or say why me? Why this?
but it makes sense
a usual thought at their expense
it makes sense, to shine as bright as the sun
and to have the balance of being less loud in
hopes of seeing the moon
when your day has just begun
sometimes I'd like to think that time knows no
bounds
and the relationships we sign our hearts to
won't waver the way we feel towards them
because it bounds us, perhaps it has grounded us
I have lived within a turbulent sea of rebellion
through gateways as high as the climb to the first
cloud
the silence up there is deafening and loud
the humming of the air, of being unbearably bare
but a lot is riding on which way to go
to fall with the knowledge or to stay with the
pain
sometimes I think it is somebody else's game
But where do we draw the line of blame?
Does it lead us anywhere closer to feeling
ashamed?
Or does it shed a good light on our names?
because there is a lot riding on my life

I feel it mostly at night
when the air is cold and my heart tries to heat
me up
I feel it sometimes during the day
but when I say it out loud, I can feel it slip away
perhaps letting go is a place I need to get to
know
buying my train ticket to life, the beauty in it
rising, seeping into the unknown.
Ever grateful for the journey I am venturing
upon.

Extinguishing the Firing Line

Behind the eyes of fluorescent sight
Limp speechless and tired from the fight
of lining up a way to be
forever in its finality
the moment in it shivers, glimmering in a light I
do not expect to understand
carefully told to grasp the inside of your hand
like I didn't know how
or where to place my love
like it wasn't enough
to be told I am even deserving of a love held true
like every part of me knew
to extinguish the firing line
like the fire of feeling fine
and the forest fire of my design
happily hopeless, but still striving to find
a peaceful bliss
surviving smoke of the near miss
maybe somewhere inside of this
we can extinguish the fire
that lives within hearts of torment
Lining up a way to be
Forever in its finality.

A Lover In The Way

As I wake, there is a lover in the way
I look closely but realise that she has been led
astray,
I try to smile to comfort her unforgiven stare
But there are people here too, I realise they
never saw you
For who you are, but for someone who was lost
I usher for them to leave but they seem not to
care
Where are we, I question her
I am the lover in the way, and you are the lover
that never stayed
Beauty bound and taken for something I am not
I treasure the world that gave me our love but
not the one that seemed to defeat it
Somehow delete it.
She starts to question me,
Where are we, the same question
I tell her that I am in a haze and that she can't
stay
She moves further back, reaches for the door
The ceiling never left, and the sky seems to
touch the floor
I feel bombarded, I feel small and alienated
She says she is leaving but the door won't move

Every other word is like a world within her
words and I feel like I can't translate
She starts pulling on the door handle.
Once it opened she stared into the Milky Way
The sparkling stars are so bright,
we are not where we thought we were,
we were immersed in a room inside the sky.
Because the sky touched the floor and there was
a lover in a way, just today.

Don't Fish In My Sea

There is beauty in the waves that rise, like the
trembling sky yet steady in our eyes
That lives above the blackened blues that is the
sea
Against my tide I take pride in knowing you
don't fish on this side
My sea is yearning for a different kind of heart
Where they live together in a work of art
Such dislocated days
It's in my silent rage that I will find solitude
again today
Don't fish in my sea
Or bankrupt my heart
Don't dream the same dreams
Because you want a fresh start
There is beauty in the course of a tale
That is told to you from birth
But don't let it be your curse
Fish somewhere else, in this vast universe
As fast as can be, and as slow as you need
Let your dreams be your own
And don't fish in my sea.

Barren Land

There is a hallway that waits for you at the end
of every day, and although it is not at the
forefront of your mind you have walked through
it an endless amount of times. It isn't dark, nor is
it light the hallway knows you best, it has never
been a test. Almost an offering, with seven doors
surrounding the narrow space, you tend to pick
up pace. The door at the end is your final
walk-through, nobody will enter it too. To be
guided by the light at every door, every
opportunity, every flawless element takes
courage within these walls, but you've never
known it consciously. For you love a barren land
that lives within you.

If Love Was Enough

I would be looking to the horizon, and thinking
maybe it's not too much
If love were enough
I would stay within the walls of his future
If enough of my love were yours
I'd not take a moment to agree but rather the
time to succeed, to take your lead
If love were reachable by phone
I'd have called you a thousand times
But enough of my love has washed up on barren
shores
For enough of my love has changed it's course
From my heart to yours
Enough of the love that I gave
Has become the object of the charade
Something changed and made
Something broken but new
You see, I have new love
Enough of it, at least
To give away
Enough to keep
Enough to save
If love was enough
I would love everyday.

On Tuesdays We Drive To The Moon

Driving the sundown and making the moon
move, further through and into the light's abyss,
did we miss any of this? Because between and
over the way we lean in for a kiss, never missing
a beat, always high off the heat, sticky torment
with loving openly adamant arms.
Your white car is parked it is glistening in the
dark, I think I can see it from where I'm standing
in a place where the moon is shining, we are so
far apart… yet I think you just drove past. Your
car is symbolic of the stars and the moon and the
way we laugh, your white car is something I just
drove past, like two forest fires, about to touch,
like the way it was just too much, I think the
ending just begun because I was fighting and it
just sung, through me, like a songbird realising
its love for life or the way we say goodnight, so
softly, ever gently. Missing you contently. On
Tuesdays, we drive to the Moon whilst our
dreams hold us in the palm of their hands.

The Hearts Door

An old man once said, have you found it yet?
And I wondered what, after years I had forgotten
to look around,
for something so aloof, staggering towards the
summit of a dream.
Left in the dust of youth, old with rust. Battered
and ashamed, but I can't say I am to blame. The
old man had a vacant stare, yet blissfully aware
that the search would never finish. Once I'd
found it the feeling in it would diminish. We
learn to love like how the stars somehow never
miss the edges of the Earth, just to include it like
they already knew it needed that, we have no say
on nature's hand yet I can't sway this little old
man into believing I had found something I had
not. The future begins at every hello and a new
chapter in every goodbye but I still can't figure
out why, this old man asks so much of me. For I
cannot look into time and foresee the ending in
this, I need a few more goodbyes in order to
determine a plot.

Light It With Hope

We live halfway between tethered memories,
and that of those we will make further along.
Down a line of a life, given moons ago. Years
will pass by, like how the sun falls each day and
in it, tries to remember your face.
Before darkness and damned dreams flutter
across the minds of the world,
we reside somewhere in the middle, we have
always done that, safe in the knowledge that
both the past and the future are the same
distance apart and that you can travel between
them, as often as you like.
You can sit with the child or hold the hand of the
elder, knowing that they are both you inside a
soul you grew. Taking up residency in your heart
before the sun falls, like a tantrum from a
toddler in the middle of a supermarket, refusing
to leave it and wishing to see its favourite toy on
one of the shelves. Just like the sun not wanting
to depart with day, knowing it would only have
to start over again come dawn, beckoning in the
sky and bargaining with the clouds. Freeing up a
mind that was mine, and casting off to a better
time. Under temperaments that sway in the
breeze and are not yet recognised. Through eyes

that flicker through days, we can only learn how to be okay. Because for as long as there has been this feeling, the notions in it won't demand a spiritual bereavement. Carefully grieving for something unchanged, for circumstances to remain the same. You have been given a bulb of light, sometimes even just to turn it on at night when the air is settled and slight, telling tales of days as long as the pain that lives in my heart, is somewhere displayed and apart. Tearing down at the walls that surround the calling I was promised. This is how we get by when we discover the sky, it is the biggest thing that exists in our lives, the vastness that propels and ponders over, the sun has always been shining too, maybe it was only ever there for you so ignite your match upon the sun and light every room with hope, because often when travelling so frequently between the past and uncertainty, we need things to help us cope, light it all with hope.

Sometimes We Wait

Under my name, you can mark me as here
but do know that sometimes I seize to be
and very unintentionally
you see, I am a part of this world
a world I don't half recognise
through these eyes of mine
so lend me yours
maybe together we can compartmentalise
because I am drowning in a sea I have worked
on myself
since I was born
with a heart that knows no depths
and a life that greets death with both pleasure
and restriction
you see
sometimes life cannot withstand the pressure of
the sea
and especially with somebody who identifies as
often seizing to be
actually, under my name, you can mark me as
gone
Because the journey to where I am has been so
unbelievably long
it has been hard, cruel and tough

nobody really knows the life I have spent
precious time on
and very unintentionally cried upon
you know
every moment that flies and swirls, stutters and
splutters before your vision
it has been crafted to do just that
your lungs have to learn its depths before you
can sing
but sometimes we have to wait
in cold corridors before any certainty can be
revealed
I've marked myself here
I made it to the icy depths of the end of
somewhere
and the beginning of somewhere else
but sometimes we have to wait,
give us patience to get through the unknown
give me love to transfer warmth to those who are
showing up
and give us life to put us in the loop, a
situational hoop
of everything we'll end up doing
sometimes we wait
but it's never too late
to love, to give, to hope.